INDIE AUTHOR CONFIDENTIAL 15

SECRETS NO ONE WILL TELL YOU ABOUT BEING A WRITER

M.L. RONN

CONTENTS

ABOUT THIS SERIES

This isn't your typical writing self-help book. This series is a compilation of lessons learned from an indie author trying to walk the path to success. Follow author M.L. Ronn (Michael La Ronn) as he navigates what it means to master the craft of writing, marketing, and running a profitable publishing business. Learn from his successes and failures, and learn about things that most successful authors only talk about behind the scenes.

To read all the collected volumes of this series in an anthology, visit www.authorlevelup.com/confidential.

INTRODUCTION

This ends an interesting year, to say the least. As I'll write later, 2023 was a good year, but not a great year. I definitely celebrated some accomplishments, but overall, I fell far short of where I wanted to be.

That's not stopping me, though. This is a jam-packed volume with a focus on writing craft this quarter. I have been reading and studying the works of mega bestsellers and capturing my learnings. I also had a breakthrough in AI editing. This breakthrough alone was my best success of the year.

In the Writing Master section, I discuss lessons learned from Michael Crichton, Clive Cussler, and more.

In the Technology and Data section, I discuss my advancements in AI editing (which were significant) and my return to fiction audiobooks.

In the Looking Forward section, I cover my commitments to improving my health and fitness, as well as major accomplishments this year. I also recap my achievements for the year and list my strategic priorities for 2024.

Overall, I have a lot to be proud of this year, but I have a lot further to go. The journey continues this quarter.

Enjoy this volume.

--*M.L. Ronn*
December 22, 2023

BECOME A WRITING MASTER

LESSONS FROM THE 6:20 MAN AND THE EDGE

This quarter, I read two books by David Baldacci: *The 6:20 Man* and *The Edge*, both in the Travis Devine series. While the novels are technically mysteries, Baldacci writes them with thriller pacing. For this reason, I consider him to be a great writer to study if you want to learn how to write mysteries and thrillers.

The 6:20 Man follows Travis Devine, an ex-Ranger who leaves the military in disgrace after an interpersonal conflict results in a colleague dying. The death wasn't Travis's fault, but he bears the heavy burden of it, submitting himself to a mental prison by going to Wall Street and working at a cutthroat financial analysis firm. He takes the 6:20 train every morning, and the story begins (and ends) on the train, hence the title of the first book. I won't give any more spoilers.

I learned a tremendous amount from reading David Baldacci. This chapter will recount the major lessons learned from both novels.

Hiding Details

. . .

When I read mystery novels, I can figure out who the killer is before the novel ends approximately 70 percent of the time. I'm not the best guesser in the world, but I do okay.

I had no idea who the killer was in this novel. Not a clue. Most readers didn't either if you look at the reviews. That's saying something. Usually, readers will brag in reviews that they knew who the killer was all along. They wear it as a badge of honor. You will *not* see that in reviews for *The 6:20 Man*. In fact, readers praised Baldacci in their reviews that the plot had more twists than a pretzel and it kept them reading. That's evidence of a master at work.

This is because Baldacci hides details with skill. Rather, he doesn't *hide* anything—he puts it out in the open and readers just miss it. He does this by fixating the viewpoint character on one or two suspects so that the reader subconsciously has to choose which one *they* think is guilty. However, none of them are guilty and this trick is mere misdirection.

It's like going to a magic show. The magician distracts your eyes while he performs the real trick in plain sight.

By giving readers a choice, it will never occur to them that the choices the writer offers are invalid.

I'm sure there is a psychological name for this. I've seen this phenomenon in my professional career in insurance. I've been in many meetings where someone presents several options for how to move forward on a project. Most people in the room will consider the options, and, unless the options are terrible, they will pick one. However, every once in a while, a person in the room will raise their hand and say, "Wait--what about X?" Such a comment usually catches the organizer off-guard; either they didn't consider it or they were intentionally omitting it.

I don't mean to be cynical, but based on how Baldacci

executed this novel, the same appears to be true with readers. He gave me a slew of choices, and I took it as an intellectual challenge to figure out which one was the best choice. Because of his skillful writing, it never dawned on me that all of the choices were wrong. The moment I thought I knew who the killer was, he twisted the narrative. Then, I thought I knew who the killer was again, and Baldacci twisted the novel a second time. All the clues were there; I just missed them.

To pull this off, you have to have a large cast of characters. If you give the readers one or two choices, this technique won't work as well.

The next question is, "How many details do you need to hide?"

The answer was not what I expected. Here is a breakdown of how Baldacci "hid" each clue per scene. I am doing this without spoilers, so pardon the vagueness.

In Scene #1, Baldacci uses the "rule of three." He introduces three characters that the main character knows, and the main character interacts with each of them. Character #1 receives somewhere around 200 words of introduction through dialogue, narrative, and action. Character #2 enters and receives around the same amount, maybe slightly less. Then, Character #3 (the killer), receives a 600-ish word stylish introduction where Baldacci uses a special technique with dialogue that I won't go into. The reason he does this is because the hero likes Character #3 and they have the deepest relationship of the three. *Immediately after the conversation* (and I mean immediately), two unrelated bad guys appear.

The amount of time Baldacci spends on the killer is the clue. Baldacci couches the clue with two misdirections. The first misdirection is the narrator mentioning that Character #3 has been living in a certain place for longer than Characters #1 and #2, which is an odd detail that stands out. The second misdirection is the bad guys who appear immediately after the conversation with Character #3. Baldacci just installed a clue by giving Character #3 the most screen time in the chapter, but the reader instead fixates on the men with guns because they're an immediate threat to Travis.

The lesson? Rule of three, minor misdirection through narrative, clue, major misdirection that threatens the hero's physical safety, end chapter on a cliffhanger.

Also, if a hero *likes* the killer, that's a fantastic way to hide details because if the hero likes someone, the reader will like them too.

In Scene #2, Baldacci uses the rule of three again. Travis chats with Character #1, then chats with Character #2, and then Character #3, who again receives the most page time. They also receive the most character description and time with Travis. There are no clues in this chapter, but curiously, Baldacci does insert the sentence, "[The killer] obviously didn't know about his dilemma." That's an interesting thing to have a narrator say. Because the narrator says it, the reader believes it, even though it is not true.

In Scene #3, the hero meets with the killer, who explains that they received the offer of a lifetime...from someone that Travis currently suspects is tied to the murder. At this point, I would never have suspected the killer because of the misdirection. In fact, Travis believes that the person making the offer is doing so to get closer to *him*, and this becomes a plot point.

In Scene #4, Travis explains that he worked out the problem with the person making the offer and that the killer is welcome to accept the offer, which makes the killer excited. Throughout the course of the conversation, Travis explains that a woman was killed in his office, sharing the crime with the killer for the first time. The killer then reveals that they knew the murder victim. That's the clue.

In Scene #5, the killer questions Travis about his relationship with the murder victim. Travis shares that he and the victim were intimate. This is in and of itself a clue. Then, the killer offers Travis three potential leads that he can follow up on to investigate the murder (there's the rule of three again), except all three leads end up being dead-ends. This is another clue. The killer then tells a lie that the reader doesn't realize is a lie until the end of the novel. Then, Travis shares another detail of his investigation with the killer.

Scene #5 is the linchpin. That's where all the evidence is. If I had to summarize it, it would be: the killer uses subterfuge to learn what the hero knows and sends him on a dead-end so that he will never suspect the killer.

In Scene #6, the hero meets with the killer, who is poised to accept the offer mentioned previously. The killer asks Travis about how the murder investigation is progressing. The hero shares the details with her openly. The killer makes a few comments that, in retrospect, are suspect. *Immediately* after this conversation, an important character shows up, ending the chapter on a cliffhanger.

In Scene #7, Travis meets the killer. The killer expresses empathy and shock at something physical that has just happened to Travis (that, ironically, had nothing to do with the killer).

In Scene #8, the killer expresses joy at accepting the offer discussed previously. The killer and Travis share a moment of happiness, but Travis feels terrible because it turns out that the person making the offer is a suspect again.

In Scene #9, Travis meets the killer, who is upset because the offer fell through (because, unbeknownst to the killer, Travis meddled in the affair).

In Scene #10, Travis introduces a female character to the killer, but the reception is chilly.

In Scene #11, the killer's fortunes turn around with a new offer, and Travis encourages them.

In Scene #12, the killer is in the hospital and Travis meets with them. He still doesn't suspect the killer.

In Scene #13, the killer finally reveals themselves and monologues about why they did what they did, letting the reader put all the pieces together.

In summary, there are 13 scenes with the killer, but there are only three scenes with clues: Scenes #1, #4, and #5. There are three clues in total. All other scenes with this character and details given are either unimportant or misleading.

This was an absolutely fascinating exercise. And I have to say it again: the novel is full of misdirection. There are many characters, and Baldacci constantly gives false clues. He gives you so many that it short-circuits your brain.

Also, it's worth pointing out that almost all of the scenes with the killer except for the final confrontation are slower-paced scenes. The hero often meets with the killer after something bad has just happened. The chapters with the killer serve as "breathing room" for the reader. This is probably another reason why I missed the clues.

Thriller readers are conditioned to expect thrills. Chapters where the hero is relaxing at home or with friends are great places to hide clues because readers typically look for clues in the thrilling sections.

If I had to replicate this technique, I would follow these steps:

1. Use a large cast of characters.
2. Misdirect the reader towards one or two suspects, and make the character focus on them.
3. Gradually introduce more suspects throughout the novel, each of them also a misdirection. I would do

this until the 95 percent mark so that readers never stop considering the false choices.

4. Meanwhile, I would hide details of the real killer in plain sight.

5. I would give three clues in total—one in the character introduction, another during an interaction with the killer, and then a final linchpin scene where it's all there for the reader.

6. To hide the details, the tools I could use to hide the details include: using the rule of three and focusing more on the killer, ending a conversation with the killer with a plot twist or cliffhanger that has nothing to do with the killer, hiding clues in slow-paced scenes, and (not covered in this chapter but useful tips I learned from other mega bestsellers), hiding clues using the passive voice or weak verbs, hiding clues in large clusters of information increase the chances of reader fatigue and readers missing them.

7. I would reveal the killer at the end of the novel. If I followed the steps above, readers won't see it coming.

The Edge

Fortunately, shortly after I wrote the first draft of this chapter, David Baldacci released *The Edge*, book two in the 6:20 *Man* series. I was excited to read it because the events and writing style of the first book were still fresh in my head.

Baldacci did not disappoint. In many ways, I liked The Edge *more* than the first book. In other ways, I did not.

First, I confirmed that my suspicions were correct. Baldacci uses the exact same technique to introduce the killer in *The Edge*. He introduces three characters in rapid succession, and—wait for it—the third character is the suspect. In this case, the third person was not the killer, but they were an accomplice who knew everything that was going on. I knew this from the very beginning, and so when Baldacci introduced all sorts of misdirection (as he is very good at doing), I saw right through the trick. That said, the mystery still had lots of twists and it kept me entertained all the same.

Something else that really struck me with this novel was the quality of the sensory writing. I don't know why, but I don't remember being blown away by the sensory details in *The 6:20 Man*. The details were great, but they didn't draw attention to themselves like they did in *The Edge*. There is just some wonderful writing throughout *The Edge*. This is because the novel takes place on the scenic coast of Maine. There are so many more opportunities to create a great setting there than in New York City where the first novel took place. This novel cemented Baldacci as one of the great sensory detail writers. Out of all of the mega bestsellers I've read so far, I would put him up there with Dean Koontz and Michael Crichton. Seriously, there were so many excellent immersive moments in this novel.

I also enjoyed the characters more in this novel. They were more endearing, had more interesting backstories, and they really felt like small-town people. In the first novel, most of the characters were unlikable, and this was due to much of the novel revolving around a cutthroat financial analyst firm. The first novel gave me the (incorrect) assumption that all of Baldacci's novels would have characters like this. I was wrong.

A final thing I noticed in this book that I also noticed in the first one was how odd Baldacci's character names are. The last name of the murder victim usually has to do with the theme of the story. In the first novel, Sarah Ewes is the murder victim. Her last name signifies her helplessness and a deeply personal situation that I won't spoil. ("Ewe" is a term for a female lamb.)

In this novel, the murder victim's name is Jenny Silkwell, which I happen to think is a great last name. Silkwell is implicated in the middle of a web of secrets and lies that pervade the small town of Putnam, Maine. I love the symbolism of the name.

However, the other last names of Baldacci characters are more head-scratching. I won't say anything more than this, but something about his character naming conventions doesn't sit well with my ear. Maybe that's intentional, but it's a distinctly Baldacci thing. I don't get this vibe with other mega bestsellers, though other mega bestsellers are known to take common names and spell them slightly differently for stylistic purposes. As a reader, this puts me on edge. As a writer, I think it's pretty cool. Just another tool for my toolbox.

In any case, I learned a lot from David Baldacci. I look forward to reading more of his novels in the future.

LESSONS FROM PACIFIC VORTEX!

I had the pleasure of reading my first Clive Cussler novel this quarter. It popped up in a recommendation after I finished listening to a Michael Crichton audiobook.

I have always wanted to read a Clive Cussler novel, so I grabbed *Pacific Vortex!*

Pacific Vortex! is the first (chronological) novel in the Dirk Pitt series, so it is not the first Dirk Pitt novel that Cussler published. In the foreword, Cussler writes that the novel is one of his weaker ones but that he hopes readers enjoy it.

I enjoyed it very much. Within a few minutes of reading, I immediately understood why Amazon recommended it to me after reading Michael Crichton. Cussler and Crichton have very similar styles. In fact, there were times when I could have sworn I was reading a Michael Crichton novel.

I've written about Michael Crichton a lot in this series. One of his biggest weaknesses as a writer was his lack of likeable characters. He excelled at weaving interesting premises and painting fantastic sensory details, but he never quite mastered creating likable (and memorable) characters. Cussler, on the other hand, shares similarities with Michael Crichton but very few of the downsides. Dirk Pitt is instantly a likeable character. Aside from a few cringing moments of mega masculinity, he embodies everything I like in a protagonist—he's good at what he does, smart, perceptive, and he makes mistakes that have real consequences.

Clive Cussler was also heavily influenced by Lester Dent's *Doc Savage* series. At times, I could have sworn I was reading a Doc Savage novel too.

Hell, even the villain in *Pacific Vortex!* is Doc Savage! He's a 6'8" tall man with mysterious golden eyes. Anyone who's read a Doc Savage novel knows that's Doc. Also, the villain acts and speaks like Doc too. I enjoyed that homage very much.

Cussler is a lot like Crichton in that he is very transparent in his writing style. His techniques are extremely easy to spot and study. That makes him an author worth paying attention to. Pound for pound, I can "see" techniques he's using more clearly than I can with other mega bestsellers.

This chapter will recap some of Cussler's techniques that I spotted so that I can record them and learn from them.

Prologues

Cussler starts every Dirk Pitt novel with a prologue where something mysterious happens. The prologue is usually set in the past and foreshadows events to come. In this case, Cussler's prologue was approximately 2,000 words. It begins with a half-abstract opening, which is an opening type where the narrator gives facts and/or opinions about the world or the lore of the world. "Half" in this sense means that the standard abstract opening is approximately 400 to 800 words; this opening was half that at only 200 to 400 words. It pivots into a standard opening, which is defined as a hero in a setting with a problem, with rich sensory details, history, and opinions of the character.

There is a stark difference between these two types of openings.

Abstract openings (also known as summary openings) are mainstays of mega-bestseller fiction. Because they are narrative-driven, they often do not contain (many) sensory details, so they are usually followed up with standard openings. That's exactly what Cussler does in this prologue.

Anyway, I was surprised to see that this prologue was only 2,000 words. Usually, I think of prologues as being slightly longer. This taught me that you can get away with a lot in a prologue and keep it short as long as you pack in the sensory details.

Extended Standard Openings

I observed an effective variation on standard openings with Cussler. In one chapter, Dirk gets ready for a mission and leaves his hotel. This is around 500-600 words, with rich sensory details. Then, he gets into his car and drives across Hawaii to a museum. The setting changes and Cussler uses more sensory details. Finally, the hero arrives at the museum, where the story resumes.

The technique I observed is what I call an extended standard.

As I wrote previously, a standard opening is a scene that takes place with a hero in a setting, with a problem, told through the five senses, character history, and opinion. It's a very specific type of opening that is instantly noticeable. There are many variables at play in a standard opening; for example, if a character has been to that setting before, they will see it differently than if they had not. If the *reader* has been to the setting before through the eyes of the character, the author will treat the setting slightly differently. The variable at play here is *familiarity*.

As a general rule, when the hero is in an unfamiliar setting, a master will take more time to set it up. When the setting is familiar, the master will take less.

In this example, Dirk Pitt was in a familiar setting (his hotel room). He (and the reader) spent the previous two chapters in it, so Cussler didn't need to spend much time establishing the setting. However, once Dirk passed from the hotel into his sports car, the setting became unfamiliar (to the reader), and Cussler immediately switches to "setting establishment mode. It was so clear and transparent that I couldn't have missed it.

The result was 500-600 words in the hotel, followed by 500-600 words traveling across Hawaii, followed by the story resuming. The opening itself is 1,000 to 1,200 words, and it is technically two openings in one.

The lesson I took away was this: when a hero transitions from a familiar to an unfamiliar setting, or vice versa, I can use an extended standard to help keep the reader grounded in the story.

Another lesson I learned was that there are rules of engagement for settings: whenever the hero enters a new setting, the writer *must* stop and establish it. The amount of time the setting receives depends on the location in the novel, the setting's familiarity, pacing, and more, but the writer *must* take time to establish a basic picture of the setting before continuing. When you look for it, you can see this at work in the novels of every mega bestseller, from Dean Koontz to John Grisham to Cassandra Clare to Clive Cussler. They all do it.

· · ·

Character Introductions

Cussler introduces his characters similarly to how Crichton does it. Whenever a new character enters the story, Cussler takes around 150 to 300 words to describe them. Sometimes he gives all the character details upfront, in what I call a "block" character introduction. Visually, all the details look like a "block" of text.

Other times, Cussler uses what I call a "layered block," which is a cluster of details followed by narrative, dialogue, or action, then another cluster, then more narrative, dialogue, or action, and a final cluster. This pattern is technically infinitely repeatable for as long as the author needs, but masters usually don't go on too long.

One example of a layered block is the introduction of the character Summer, the love interest du jour. When Dirk sees her for the first time, he focuses on her eyes. Then, the narrative focuses on his reaction to her beauty. After that, we get more details, followed by dialogue. And repeat.

The layered block is extremely effective and if it weren't for Cussler, I might have missed this technique in other novels.

Media Inserts

In the second chapter, Dirk reads a letter from the deceased captain of a missing submarine, and Cussler's treatment of it is masterful. He gives the reader around 200-300 words of the letter, pauses for Dirk's reaction, then continues the letter. The result is an attractive, layered narrative where the letter is woven organically with dialogue, narrative, and action.

As I said, this is exactly something Crichton would do. I might try this same technique one day.

Head Hopping

There are several instances of head hopping in the novel. Of the three I remembered, one of them works brilliantly; the other two do not. This taught me a lot.

In the instances that do not work, they happen at the end of a chapter where Cussler jumps into the head of a supporting character who marvels at how smart Dirk Pitt is. That's it. There are no sensory details or any other reasons for doing this other than to have the supporting character express admiration for Dirk. To me, this is why the head-hop didn't work.

In the instance where it worked very well, Dirk and a navy diver infiltrate a sunken submarine, and they discover that the submarine is fully operational. The chapter ends, and the narrative shifts to a supporting character at a naval base who discovers that Dirk is communicating with them through the sunken submarine, which amazes him. This scene is told through the viewpoint of the supporting character, and combined with Dirk's success and charm, it works well. The pacing in this chapter is also fast.

The lesson I learned was that you can get away with head-hopping if the scene is fast-paced or there is a big emotion (like success). The pacing anesthetizes the reader, making them less likely to pick up on the fact that you head-hopped. And if they do, they won't mind because you just gave them a thrill.

In *The Andromeda Strain* by Michael Crichton, he does something very similar at the end of the novel where he jumps between characters during the final battle. The pacing is frenzied and the reader is turning the page with lightning speed during this section of the novel. This is precisely why Crichton gets away with it.

Again, this is why Cussler and Crichton are cut from the same cloth. They use techniques in a similar manner, and they solve problems the same way.

Bringing It All Together

Overall, Cussler is one of my new favorite writers. He wrote that he didn't think *Pacific Vortex!* was his best novel, but I thought it was pretty darn good. Sure, it wasn't perfect, but no novel is, really. I can't wait to see what Cussler reads like at the top of his game.

LESSONS FROM EATERS OF
THE DEAD

My imaginary mentorship with Michael Crichton continues. This quarter, I read *Eaters of the Dead*, a short but mighty novel written by Michael Crichton in the late 70s. I bought the book sight unseen and had no idea what to expect. I didn't even read the book description. I just trusted that Crichton would tell a great story and teach me something in the process. Boy, was I right.

Eaters of the Dead is a first-person narrative retelling of Beowulf. It recounts the story of Ibn Fadlan, an Arabic traveler who visits Scandinavia in the year 922. During his travels, he recounts his journeys with a band of Norsemen, specifically Beowulf. The Norsemen fight creatures of the mist (Grendels) and slay Mother Grendel. Ibn Fadlan was a real person who did visit Scandinavia, but Crichton fictionalizes the account and takes some authorial liberties.

Honestly, I went into this novel with skewed expectations. I expected the usual Crichton fare—science, scientific characters, the usual fiction techniques that I describe all the time in this series, and so on. That's not what I got.

The entire novel is a masterclass in how to tell stories in the old style. By "old-style," I mean telling stories around the camp-fire. The narrative style reminded me of Alexis de Tocqueville's *Democracy in America*, in which the Frenchman traveled across the United States during the late 1800s and described his experiences. At other times, the narrative style reminded me of *The Arabian Nights*. While there is dialogue, it is recalled by the narrator. All "scenes" are really just memories of the narrator.

In other words, this novel was completely out of left field from what I expected, and, in the hands of a lesser author, it might have fallen flat. While it wasn't perfect, it taught me a lot.

First, I forgot how much I enjoyed *Beowulf*. I read it in high school (on my own—not as a college assignment, believe it or not), and I enjoyed it a lot. Honestly, I enjoyed it a lot more than *The Iliad* or *The Odyssey*. It has real heart, and though it was an epic poem, it exemplifies the structure of an adventure novel. I enjoyed revisiting the characters of Beowulf, Hrothgar, and Grendel, and it took me back to those pleasant days in high school when I read a ton of random books.

Here are the most important craft lessons I learned from this book.

I would wager that 70 to 80 percent of this novel is narrative. It's exactly what legions of writers say you shouldn't do—tell, not show. Yet, it's funny how mega bestsellers repeatedly prove that this commonly accepted advice can be wrong. "Telling, not showing" shouldn't be anathema; it should be a tool. And every tool has its time and place. This is a great example of why you should study the works of the mega bestsellers to see for yourself what the true unwritten rules of writing are rather than believing everything someone tells you.

Crichton's narrative is also rich with sensory details. In fact, there were many instances throughout the novel where he was still following the tried-and-true practice of using the five senses to set up a setting. I observed that every time the narrator arrived at a new setting, he described it with at least three of the five senses. The novel abounds with rich sight, sound, texture, and smell details that kept me grounded even though the narrator was telling and not showing. (I suppose you could make an argument that Crichton was showing, but he was doing it in a very telling sort of way.)

What's fascinating about this novel is that Crichton used the same techniques that he uses in all of his other novels. For example, when he introduces a character, he typically does it in a block, as I described in the chapter on Character Introductions. In *Sphere*, he introduces many of his characters with a block of description that is approximately 150 to 300 words, similar to how Crichton often does it. Then he develops the character gradually throughout the novel.

He does the same thing and *Eaters of the Dead*. For example, when he meets the Norsemen for the first time, he describes the race generally, noting their physical attributes. Then, he describes their mannerisms and customers. This is precisely what he would do in a typical novel as well. So, the only difference is that he's doing it in the first person primarily through narrative. This was a really interesting find because I would have thought the rules of writing a novel like this would have been different, or that he would have had to adopt a different style, but if you look closely, the hallmarks of his style are there.

I take from this exercise the following lesson: no matter what your narrative style or content, the five senses never go out of style. When you are writing a scene through narrative, it is especially important to use the five senses to keep the reader turning the page.

The second lesson I learned from this novel was the "shape" of the text. Throughout the entire novel, Crichton uses short paragraphs that are approximately two to four sentences in length. There are exceptions, but those are rare. The sentences he uses are approximately medium to long, with more commas and semicolons than what you would typically see in contemporary fiction. These two attributes combined help to give the narrative a steady pace.

The short paragraphs keep the reader moving down the page and they give the illusion of movement. The medium to long sentences give the paragraph color. The chapters are also not very long. The longest is somewhere around 6,500 words, which is fairly long by contemporary standards, but most of the chapters are somewhere around 2,000 to 4,000 words. I also think that this helped me maintain an interest level throughout reading.

My takeaway from this is that if I have long sections of narrative, I may want to adopt this "shape" to keep readers moving down the page (and turning the page). When writing stories with thick sections of narrative, I think the default for many writers is to use big paragraphs. That's precisely what Crichton does *not* do.

There were some other interesting anachronisms with the text that I enjoyed very much, like Crichton's use of archaic vocabulary words, but I can't really study that. I can only admire his ability to mold himself into a completely different type of novel than what he would typically write.

I love risk-taking in novels. I love to see authors do unusual things. Reading *Eaters of the Dead* was a fun read, and the book is definitely memorable in a catalog of an author who exemplifies taking chances.

LESSONS FROM CITY OF BONES

This quarter, I read *City of Bones* by Cassandra Clare. As a stalwart of urban fantasy, the book has been on my radar for years, but I never got around to reading it until now.

Overall, the book taught me quite a lot about how to do things right and how to do things wrong. I believe Clare has become a much better writer over the last ten years—she's written a lot more books since this one, but this is where it all started, and that's fascinating to me. Based on this book alone, I'd consider her to be a master in the making, but she's one that people overlook. Some of that has to do with her history writing Harry Potter fanfiction, which I won't go into here. But as a writer, she is certainly one that I learned a lot from.

I'll start with the positive lessons learned.

First, she did a fantastic job in developing a headstrong but very likable heroine in Clary Fray. Clary was instantly likable, and there were many moments throughout the manuscript where I found myself thinking, "I should do something similar with my heroes."

But why was Clary Fray likable? It was her character opinions. Clare does a terrific job of capturing character opinions.

The moments when I liked Clary the most were when Clare was giving Clary's opinions through narrative. I felt like I was inside the head of a teenage girl.

When a character voices their opinion, it is done through narrative or dialogue. Narrative opinions are far more effective because they connect directly to the reader; character opinions through dialogue are also effective but work differently. Clare figured this out, and it's one of her biggest strengths.

I reviewed the first quarter of the book and highlighted every instance of character opinion, analyzing how it made me feel. I took away some key lessons that I can apply to my next novel.

Second, Clare uses a symphony of descriptions. In particular, she does some excellent work with color. Instead of blue, she uses "electric blue." Every time she used a color, she tied it to a bright bold shade, which just worked for me. It made me question my own skill in this area—am I being this descriptive with color? If not, I need to be!

Also, Clare's descriptions are worth mentioning because they're another of her greatest strengths. There are some fantastic sensory details in this book. She uses sensory details that rival many mega bestsellers (except Dean Koontz).

That said, this is one of the reasons why I call her a "master in the making." Some of her images are excellent, but some don't work. When they don't work, they *really* don't work. Throughout reading the story, I kept thinking about the analogy of a loose cannon. A loose cannon still hits targets. Such is Clare's writing style. It's powerful, but at times too powerful. Examples of sensory images that didn't work included (paraphrased):

- He had a voice like honey poured over glass shards
- He grabbed a swag of curtains.

- A dusty sigh.
- He sighed, the shadows under his eyes becoming more pronounced.

I have no idea what honey over glass shards has to do with someone's voice.

A "swag" is not a term used to describe a curtain. A swag is actually the uppermost part of a window treatment, so it's not something you can grab easily. In the example, the character is pulling the curtain so he can look out the window.

If someone is exhaling dust when they sigh, something is seriously wrong with them.

And finally, no person in real life would be so observant as to notice the shadows under someone's eyes becoming more pronounced.

All of these are bad images that pull the reader out of the story. They're almost—dare I say it—too descriptive.

Yet, so many of Clare's sensory details are so good that I didn't mind the occasional strike. In fact, I admired her moxie. That said, either she needed a better editor or she ignored her editor's advice. We'll never know.

In any case, this was a reminder for me to be careful about being distracting with my sensory details. Other mega best-sellers don't make these kinds of mistakes. Their writing is far more controlled and precise. As of 2007 when *City of Bones* was published, Clare hadn't refined this skill yet. I'd like to read one of her newer books to see how she has progressed.

Now, I'll move on to the negative lessons.

First, the novel suffers from same chapter-length issues that I noticed with *Pacific Vortex!* The chapters are entirely too long. However, the chapter *endings* are fine. It's just that a single chapter should have been two or three chapters instead. That would have improved the pacing, especially at the middle and end of the novel, where the chapter lengths almost pulled me out of the novel.

Seeing the chapter breaks in this novel helped me confirm that my method of shorter, punchier chapters is an effective pacing tool. As a reader, they keep me turning the pages faster. As a writer, they help me keep the story cleaner.

Second, the novel was also a good lesson in how not to write a male character. Female readers complain about how some male writers write terrible female protagonists; the opposite is also true, but I don't hear anyone complain about that.

My observations:

- The love interest of the story is a jerk and treats the heroine badly (not a surprise; this is typical romance fare).
- He calls a cab driver an imbecile during a cab ride.
- He calls the heroine an idiot at least once in the novel.
- He is just generally a jerk throughout the story, with no "soft interior" that many hard-ass romance male heroes have.

And that's just the start.

A critical part of writing a male hero is making him a *man* (or at least, a man-in-training). The actions above make him abusive, which is the opposite of being a man. And then Clare made the mistake of making him the heroine's brother—after working hard to develop a romance that culminates in a beautiful kissing scene.

I have read enough romance to know that this is a no-no. Readers in reviews didn't like it either.

Second, the audiobook version of *City of Bones* is a masterclass in how not to create audiobooks. I don't know how much of what I am going to describe is Clare's fault, so I will default to blaming the publisher instead.

The audiobook narrator that I listened to had a great voice and was not unpleasant to listen to. However, she performed bad British accents, which 1) were off-putting and 2) made no sense because it was never obvious to me that some of the characters even needed British accents because the story takes place in New York. This was a bad directorial call on the part of the publisher.

Even worse, the publisher replaced the narrator with another for Book 2, and yet another for Book 3. This is unacceptable. It's one thing if a narrator passes away and cannot record future books in the series, but changing the narrator every time is a disservice to the reader because they can never adapt to the narrator. They can't hear the character's voices properly. Plus, what if they really like the first narrator but dislike the second? Or what if the third narrator is the best, but readers will never know it because the first two are so bad? The entire series needs to be rerecorded with one good narrator. It would improve the audiobook sales considerably, and it would also improve the audiobook listening experience. But I digress.

In any case, I believe Cassandra Clare is a better writer than many give her credit for. While *City of Bones* wasn't perfect, it kept me reading, and for that, Cassandra Clare remains an author to study.

LESSONS FROM PIRATE LATITUDES

My reading appetite has been insatiable this quarter. I read *Pirate Latitudes* by Michael Crichton. The novel takes place in 1665 in Jamaica, following a privateer (read: pirate) attempting to rob a Spanish fortress near the island of Jamaica on behalf of the King of England.

As with every Crichton novel I read, I learned something. Here is a summary.

The Character Reputation Introduction

There is a Spanish warship captain who is so notorious that the reader meets him long before he ever shows up on the page. He is mentioned several times in dialogue, and each time, a savage story is told about him. By the time he appears, that makes him all the more menacing.

I studied this introduction, as it was quite effective.

. . .

Painting a Picture with the Setting

Crichton uses a simple technique when introducing a character that I liked a lot. The hero is taken hostage on a Spanish warship and is taken to the Spanish captain for questioning. When the hero enters the captain's quarters, Crichton paints it with rich sensory details—around twelve in total. The final image Crichton gives is the captain, sitting in a plush velvet chair.

I liken this technique to someone looking around a room, and the person in the room is the last thing they see. Again, very effective and something I will use one day.

Assembling the Team

One of the most prominent elements of *Pirate Latitudes* is the team. Captain Charles Hunter surrounds himself with a seedy gang of pirates. In Chapter 7, Hunter visits each member to recruit them for the voyage, and each character gets their own mini introduction. Crichton uses section breaks to cordon off each introduction. It works beautifully.

Granted, Crichton doesn't do the best job of introducing the characters (this was a posthumous work, so he wasn't in full form), but the technique itself was sound.

Hero Microfocusing

There is a scene where the team has to climb a treacherous cliff in order to reach the Spanish fortress they are searching for.

However, there is an approaching storm, and if they don't climb immediately, they'll never make it. What ensues is a fantastic scene where the hero follows his party up the cliff. It's high stakes, high tension, and Crichton uses masterful sensory detail to put the reader inside Hunter's head as he climbs, not knowing whether he will live or die.

Form-wise, Crichton uses medium paragraphs and longer sentences, which is the opposite of what I expected. But when I thought about it, it made sense. Crichton wants you to stay deep inside Hunter's head. The longer sentences and paragraphs draw out the conflict.

It reminded me of a story I heard about Navy SEALs training. It's some of the most rigorous training in the world. In the training, there's a concept called "microfocus." The candidates who focus on passing the training usually fail. The candidates who focus on the moment at hand, however, usually pass. Instead of thinking, "What can I do to pass the training?" they instead ask, "What can I do to move my arm while I'm crawling under barbed wire in the mud in the middle of a thunderstorm?" In microfocusing, you focus on the task at hand.

I think Crichton is making the character do the same thing and letting the reader experience it. He uses many "touch" details so that the readers themselves also feel like they're on the cliffside with Hunter.

Posthumous Woes

Pirate Latitudes was published posthumously shortly after Michael Crichton's death. Crichton's posthumous novels have a bad reputation, one that I had heard about long before I read this book. Now I see why. However, the novel wasn't *terrible*.

I enjoyed *Pirate Latitudes* for the same reasons I enjoy Crichton's other novels he wrote while he was alive. Great premise, incredible sensory details, and gripping action. The parts I enjoyed, I really enjoyed.

The things I disliked about the novel were the same things I disliked about Crichton's ante mortem books. He doesn't write female characters well. Sometimes he gets a little too bogged down in technical details. And, his characters could be much better.

Ironically, the cast in *Pirate Latitudes* was one of his better casts. It would have been his best cast of characters if it weren't for the awful last half of the book.

And that leads me to an issue I've noticed with Crichton's writing. He starts his novels strong, but they don't always end strong. I had this same problem with *Sphere*. *Sphere* would have been my favorite Crichton novel if he hadn't killed off the great cast he built around the halfway mark.

In *Pirate Latitudes*, the first half of the novel is excellent and as good as anything Crichton's ever written. There are some issues here and there with the writing, but the story and characters are, for the most part, solid. But I could tell that Crichton must have only written this novel up to around the halfway mark, because the tone and writing style changes significantly after the heroes raid the Spanish fortress and make off with the treasure they were looking for.

At this point, the novel should have just ended with them sailing back to Jamaica. But that's not what happens. We get an odd battle with a Spanish warship, an encounter with cannibals, a hurricane, and, strangely, a battle with a sea kraken. Even worse, these sections are largely devoid of strong sensory detail that Crichton typically uses. It feels like the publisher padded the novel for profit.

The "final battle" upon returning home to Jamaica is also

weak. Again, Crichton doesn't write the best endings, but I don't think he actually wrote this one. I've read enough of him to know his style very well. I feel strongly that the last half of the novel was not written by him.

That said, I still enjoyed the novel overall and it was a good time. I didn't study it too much because it's not Crichton at his best. However, it's still worth reading because there is some great writing in the first part of the novel.

IMPROVING MY VOCABULARY A LA DEAN KOONTZ

I've written in previous volumes of this series about my admiration for Dean Koontz and his use of the English language. There is no writer like him. He is by far the best practitioner of the English language. The way he uses words is nothing short of mesmerizing. If I can be a fraction as good as he is in this area, then I'll be somebody.

Yet, so many writers fall into the trap of focusing on "pretty words." Trust me, I'm not falling into that trap. I want to choose words that are going to create images in readers' heads, make the black words on the page disappear, and exercise mind control. Nothing more, nothing less.

If you read Dean Koontz (and to a lesser extent, other mega bestsellers), you can break his word usage into different patterns:

- unique and arresting words
- unique and arresting phrases
- descriptive words that the average person would probably never use in a sentence but would instantly understand based on context

I am interested in learning how to master all three of these elements, but for the purposes of the exercise I am going to describe, I focused solely on the third category: descriptive words and phrases that the average person would never use in a sentence but would instantly understand based on the context. This primarily involves calling things by their proper names, which we don't often do.

For example, when the average person describes something, they say "window." They don't say casement window, double-hung window, arched window, stained-glass window, or leaded casement. However, with the exception of leaded casement, you probably understood exactly what I was talking about when I used the more descriptive words. That's the beauty of mega-bestseller word usage. As a general rule, this is precisely where I want to be operating 100 percent of the time when I'm writing.

There's also the problem of false details. When one says "window," it can create trouble for the writer if they don't describe it specifically. For example, if I say that my main character stood next to the window, and then several paragraphs later, I suggest that the window can be pulled upward to open, suggestive of a paned window, what if the reader had an image of a casement (a window that you crank to open) in their head? Well, I just pulled the reader out of the story. The use of the unadorned term "window" created this false detail and worked against the spirit of the story. This is the sort of thing you must desperately try to avoid as a writer. When it happens, readers aren't "seeing" the story unfold as a series of images in their minds; they are seeing the black marks on the page again. If there's anything you don't want them to see, it's black marks on the page. You've got to get those black marks to disappear. Most mid-list and best-selling authors have managed to master using descriptive language, so this isn't a problem for most successful authors. However, Dean Koontz simply takes this to another level entirely. I want to be at *that* level.

How do I do it?

I experimented with a new technique. It happened on a whim.

My daughter loves to go to the public library. I take her there once or twice a month so she can check out books. She reads them so quickly that sometimes I take her to the library every week! (I love this about my daughter and I hope this isn't a phase that she grows out of!)

Anyway, my daughter was browsing the children's book section and I wandered the stacks to the nonfiction aisles. This particular library has a lot of items from the 1970s, 1980s, 1990s, and early 2000s. The librarians have excellent taste because they love to stock books on very specific subjects that have lots of pictures.

As an author and someone who deals exclusively in the written word, it might sound silly that I want books with pictures to help me understand things, but it's just true. Pictures help you understand what things are. They also help you understand how to call things by their names.

I checked out four of the most random books I could find:

- a book about window treatments
- a book about room makeovers
- a book about motorized scooters
- a book about rugby

Each of these books was written by subject matter experts in this field and tailored for the layperson who had very little understanding about the topic at hand. These were the perfect books to help me learn about a new subject while also learning the proper names of things and how to describe them.

I started with the window treatments book. I skimmed the book, reading it lightly and focusing on words that met the criteria I just described: they had to be words the average person would understand either instantly or by context. I wasn't interested in words that would make readers reach for the dictionary.

I thought I would find about a dozen or so words in this book. I found far more than that—around 300. As I skimmed through the book, I turned on my voice recorder and dictated the words and phrases I wanted to capture. Then, I transcribed the audio, which was around 90 percent accurate. After cleaning it up, I had a list of 300 words that I never would have used in a sentence previously. These words were Dean Koontz level. I was simply flabbergasted at *how many* words there were.

Next, I went to work with the focus of being able to recall these words more easily so that I can import them into a work of fiction down the road if desired. On a Microsoft OneNote file, I created a table with several columns:

- objects
- verbs
- words that denoted opinion—in other words, words a narrator or viewpoint character might use when describing windows or window treatments
- sensory details

Then, I took each word and slotted it into the appropriate section and alphabetized each section.

Some words needed pictures to support them, so I created a reference table with images of words that I didn't quite understand to help me be able to describe them in the future.

I also took pictures on my phone of images from the book and placed them in the OneNote file as well.

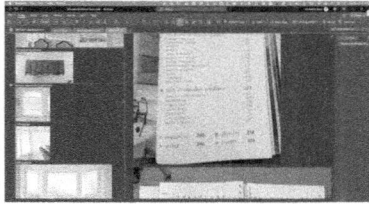

When I was done, I had an amazing reference that I could use whenever I came to a scene where I needed to describe a window. I spent the time to build this 1) because it was the first time I had done this exercise and 2) you'd be amazed how often windows come up in fiction. I knew this would be useful for me down the road. The phrases I captured are exactly the sort of words and phrases that Dean Koontz would use.

Now, admittedly, the other three books didn't spawn as many words as the window book did, and I'm not so sure how frequently I will ever describe scooters or rugby, the point isn't *entirely* to record words for every subject matter. The point is to exercise my muscles and expose myself to as many words and phrases as possible. They will inevitably, organically manifest themselves in my fiction whether I refer to the documents in the future or not.

Yes, I know that this work is tedious. But just imagine with me if I did this once or twice a month. Let's say I picked a completely different subject matter every time. And let's say that each exercise yielded me 100 words on average. In one year, I would know approximately 1,200 new words and phrases. How many words are in English language? I'm too lazy to look it up for this chapter, but I suspect it's in the hundreds of thousands. However, the Koontzian words probably don't number more than 100,000. Honestly, they probably don't number more than 10,000. Therefore, if my assumption is correct, in ten years, I would exercise a vocabulary similar to Dean Koontz's.

It needn't take ten years to get the benefit of such a dynamic vocabulary, however. I would likely notice the benefits much, much sooner than that—likely within a few months. In the short term, such an exercise would be a quick win; in the long term, it would be total and complete mastery. That's intoxicating to think about...

I took this exercise a little further as well. I found a website that provides a list of random words. Some of the words are basic, some of the words are intermediate, and some of the words are advanced. I set a timer for ten minutes and performed the following exercise. First, I generated a batch of approximately 100 random words. Then, I put those words in a split screen with the Microsoft OneNote documentation I described previously. I then embarked on a mind-bending exercise to pair as many of the random words with the captured words in arresting and unusual ways. The goal was to do this in a way that Dean Koontz might.

Here were some of the examples from this exercise. They are a mixture of words and phrases and are rough sketches not intended for publication in a novel without some tweaking:

- The double-hung windows were insulated as a buffer against deafening highway drone a few yards away, but even the insulation didn't block out the din of cars and semis speeding down I-70.

- A shapely Greek urn perched in front of an arched window with drawn cellular shades.
- A dapper window treatment.
- The sheer melted away on a summery day into the garden outside.
- The golden dress drapes, bronze pillars, and marble floors in the bathroom reminded me of the glory of Ancient Rome.
- Sheers swaying in the breeze next to an opening window.
- Damask wallpaper engraved into my mind's eye.
- I cranked open the casement windows, and the room sucked in cold air.
- The gold-fringed tassel tiebacks, the final grace note against the symphony of this 1800s period room.
- Unendurable luxury.
- The curtains were stamped with a playful pattern that reminded me of forward seek buttons on a radio.
- Nebulous starry sky beyond the bay window.
- A craven designer who didn't bother to finish the garden window—not even a ruffled drape or privacy curtain covered the little porthole window in the garage.
- A monochrome viridian toile fabric of trees, water, and a park—how New York must have looked like before the turn of the century.
- Drapes that pooled on the floor had run amok across the length of the window since the window was open and the weather had taken a windy turn.
- Teeny-tiny half-round window in the ceiling.
- Round window in the attic that flipped and swung like a flapjack when you opened it.

- The floor-to-ceiling windows morphed into skylights that sloped over the kitchen, spilling bars of moonlight over the granite island.
- Classically elegant farmhouse dormer windows.
- Ludicrous as café shutters in a basement window, but it worked.
- Zippy blinds.
- Quartz window sill.
- The curtains had the texture of a burlap sack but were no doubt an elegant statement in this laidback country cottage.
- Storm-colored curtains.
- Folded shutters.
- Adorned with fetching floral linen fabric.
- Clumsy contrasting colors.
- Apricot jam and nautical blue.
- Bold and sassy color palettes.
- Rich, fowl-feathered ethnic print.

Were the results stellar? Not exactly, but the goal is to exercise the muscle—nothing more, nothing less. By exercising my brain to make new and unusual associations, that will encourage it to do more of that task in the future, especially when I am writing. I very much consider this to be like performance training. An athlete practices and practices until the big day arrives to play their next game. How the athlete performs in the moment that matters is dependent entirely on how well they trained. This exercise was no more than strength and endurance training for my writing muscles.

I will try to implement this exercise on a regular basis. While one or two bouts of it may not get me incredible results, it's the cumulative effect that I ultimately want.

Very cool.

SHORT STORY FOLLOW-UP

In the previous volume of the series, I discussed a lesson learned while submitting short stories to anthologies. The gist of that chapter was that I made a mistake in how I tracked my short story submissions, and I accidentally made a simultaneous submission to multiple editors. Neither magazine explicitly discouraged simultaneous submissions, but I go out of my way to avoid this because it's not a professional look. However, it was an honest mistake that I have easily corrected so that it won't happen again.

So, what happened?

I'm pleased to inform you that my story "The Goddess of Crime" was accepted for publication in the *Hidden Villains: Betrayed* anthology, slated for publication in mid-2024. It was such a cool feeling to receive an acceptance email in my inbox.

After I finalized the acceptance, signed the contract, and settled on a few minor details with the editor, it was time to put my plan into action.

I immediately emailed the other editor of the anthology to which I had submitted the story. In a very brief email, I explained that the story had been accepted by another publication and that I needed to withdraw it. I ended the email by thanking the editor for her time and letting her know that I also had a sister story set in the same universe with a similar cast of characters, and that the story was available for review if she was interested. It was October 2023 and the editor had previously stated that she wouldn't even begin looking at the slush pile until early 2024 anyway.

To my luck, the editor replied almost immediately, congratulated me on the acceptance elsewhere, and advised me to send the other story. Awesome!

Disaster averted, one short story accepted, and another story under consideration. I'll update future volumes of the series if the second story, "The Goddess of Justice" is accepted, because that would be a pretty cool accomplishment. The stories are set in the same universe, follow two sisters on strange adventures through strange lands, and I had a blast writing them. It would be a great credit to claim that both stories were accepted for publication. But I digress.

The acceptance to the *Hidden Villains: Betrayed* anthology required some work on my part. The editors used a Kickstarter campaign to help fund the publication (and the Kickstarter was successful). I wrote a newsletter in support of the Kickstarter, shared it on my socials, and recorded a quick YouTube video announcement sending my subscriber base to the page. I created another newsletter for when the anthology was published. I also created a page on my website with links to all the major retailers so that it was ready to go live when the anthology was published. I also promoted the anthology on my monthly livestream Power Hour.

I had all of this in place less than a week after acceptance. This way, I could set it and forget it. Well, I couldn't *forget* it, but at least I knew I was carrying my weight in the anthology's marketing efforts. There was another cool experiment that I did while helping to promote this anthology. The editor asked the contributing authors to record a quick one- to two-minute video of the author reading the opening of the short story. They would post these videos on their Facebook page.

I really, really don't like author readings. I find them boring, tedious, and I don't think readers like them all that much. But hey, if an editor asks me to do something, I'm going to do it, so I found a way to make it fun and interesting.

I recorded a basic video introducing myself, a bit of background about me, a link to my site, and the name of my short story. I then read the first minute of the story per the editor's requirements.

I watched a few Facebook videos prior to recording this video, and I realized that when most people see a Facebook video, it is muted by default. If the user is interested, they must click on the video in order to turn on the sound. This got me thinking: if I'm just talking, *no one* (and I mean no one) is going to give two hoots. Instead, what if I created subtitles? This way, users can engage with the video without having to click for sound.

I did a quick web search for a video subtitle service, and I literally clicked on the first search result I found, which was a website called Cleared the Oh. Cleo made it unbelievably easy to create subtitles. I uploaded the video and the program took care of the rest. The program uses artificial intelligence to listen to my voice and create subtitles. It also allows you to edit any mistakes that the AI makes directly on the screen. In less than five minutes, I had professional subtitles at the bottom of the video. It only cost me $10. I had to pay for a one-month subscription to get access to the service, but given that I'm being paid for this short story, it was a worthy investment. I canceled the subscription immediately after the editor accepted the video.

In the future, I will know how to create good-looking subtitles for my videos if I ever need to. Experimenting with technology made the process of creating the reading and editing it more fun. The entire process took me approximately 90 minutes.

Anyway, that's what happened with my short story "The Goddess of Crime." I'm proud to have a publication credit under my name, and I look forward to seeing how the anthology performs.

But most importantly, I'm going to continue writing more stories.

DISCOVERING THE POWER OF
MIRROR NEURONS

This quarter, I took an online on-demand class from Cat Rambo, a best-selling author and previous president of the Science Fiction Writers Association (SFWA). Cat is an accomplished author, speaker, and workshop facilitator. The title of her course was "Dunking Readers in the Details," which I was able to complete in less than an hour. It's quite short, but quite powerful.

Something that Cat mentioned offhand in the video intrigued me to no end. She mentioned that pulp writers often recommended writing in the five senses (no surprise there). However, she mentioned that there is some basis in science for doing this. There is a neuron called a mirror neuron. When an author describes something that makes the reader feel it, they truly can feel it. In the course, Cat argues that this is why touch is the most important sense of all. If you can activate readers' mirror neurons, you can keep them reading.

As I said, she makes this comment offhand, and serious writers should take the course to gain all of her insights. However, I find that when I take courses from professional writers, the offhand comments are the ones that teach me more than the content of the course itself. Professional writers know so much, but they cannot share it all. Of course, it's really just a window into their world.

I began researching mirror neurons and what scientists had to say about them. I spent one day learning everything I could learn about these neurons. Below are the lessons I learned.

Mirror neurons are a class of neurons that were first discovered in the early 1990s by a team of researchers led by Giacomo Rizzolatti at the University of Parma in Italy. They began by studying the motor cortex of monkeys, which is responsible for controlling hand and mouth movements. While conducting experiments, researchers noticed that some neurons fired when monkeys performed an action *and* when they saw someone else perform the same action.

The phrase mirror neurons was created to explain this mirroring effect, where the neuron reflects the activity seen in others as if the observer were doing the action themselves. Or, you could call it the "monkey see, monkey do" neurons. This discovery challenged traditional views that neurons in the brain were primarily involved in controlling motor actions and raised intriguing questions about the neural basis of social cognition.

Mirror neurons are very important for understanding and copying what other people do. Scientists think they help us learn and behave in social situations. The discovery was first made in relation to motor actions, but later research found that it also applies to emotional and cognitive processes. These neurons are not only found in the motor cortex but can also be found in other areas of the brain such as the parietal and premotor cortices.

Though often debated, some scientists believe that mirror neurons have an important role in empathy. The theory is this: when we see someone feeling an emotion, our brain may simulate that emotion, allowing us to understand and feel the same way. This capacity for emotional resonance is fundamental to human social interactions and the development of empathy, compassion, and a sense of connectedness.

The process of learning is also affected by mirror neurons. People can learn new things more easily by copying others. This has significant implications for education, as it suggests that observational learning, or learning by watching others, is a powerful mechanism for acquiring knowledge and skills.

Additionally, mirror neurons have been connected to comprehending intentions and forecasting the actions of others. It is important to be able to predict and understand what other people want and mean in order to have good social interactions. Mirror neurons contribute to this by allowing individuals to simulate and understand the actions of others at a deeper level.

Courtesy of the ChatGPT and Claude AI chatbots, here are some interesting tips they gave me for activating my mirror neurons in my writing.

1. Let readers infer intentions. Allow readers to comprehend your characters' intentions and predict their actions through context, dialogue and behaviors. Their brains' mirroring properties fill in the gaps, keeping them engaged.

2. Use empathy and resonance. Have moments where characters deeply understand others' emotions or situations. This emotional resonance taps into the proposed link between mirror neurons and empathy.

3. Include examples of observational learning. Show your characters learning new information or skills by watching someone else. This reflects the role mirror neurons play in social learning.

4. Consider the brain science. Know key mirror neuron research so your depictions of cognition, behavior and interaction align with how brains actually operate.

5. Use vivid and detailed descriptions that engage the senses. When describing actions or emotions, provide sensory details that allow readers to visualize, feel, and experience the scenes. This activates readers' mirror neurons by simulating the experiences in their minds.

6. Develop well-rounded characters with relatable emotions and experiences. By portraying characters' emotional states and reactions realistically, readers can connect with and understand the characters on a deeper level. This connection may be facilitated by the activation of mirror neurons.

7. Explore the concept of observational learning in your storytelling. Show characters learning and growing through observation, whether it's acquiring new skills, understanding social dynamics, or navigating emotional situations. This aligns with the idea that mirror neurons contribute to learning through imitation.

8. Craft scenes that evoke empathy by describing characters' emotions in a way that allows readers to feel a similar emotional resonance. This can help readers relate to the characters and their experiences, fostering a stronger connection.

9. Incorporate tactile sensations into your writing. Describing the texture of objects, the warmth of a hug, or the sensation of a gentle breeze can activate readers' mirror neurons. Touch is a powerful sense

that can evoke emotional responses and create a more immersive reading experience.

10. Pay attention to the emotional nuances in dialogue. Reflect characters' emotions through their words, tone, and body language. This not only deepens the emotional impact of your writing but may also engage readers' mirror neurons as they empathize with the characters.

11. Experiment with a variety of descriptive language to convey emotions and actions. Avoid repetitive or clichéd expressions. Use fresh and evocative language to stimulate readers' imaginations and enhance the mirror neuron response.

12. Engage multiple senses in your descriptions. Incorporate sounds, smells, and tastes to create a rich sensory experience. This approach can contribute to a more holistic activation of readers' mirror neurons.

In summary, Cat Rambo is absolutely correct that touch is the most important sense of all. It's backed by science. Moving forward, I'm going to pay more attention to touch than I currently do (and currently, I pay attention to it a lot). When I use touch details, I will use details that increase the chances of activating readers' mirror neurons. These details must also be filtered through the point of view character's senses. This is harder than it sounds, and it requires a workmanlike approach. That also got me thinking about what the "workmanlike approach" would look like for the other senses. Are there studies on taste, sound, and smell, for example? This is all fascinating, and relatively uncharted territory. Hopefully, I can explore it in a future volume of this series.

PREPARING FOR SUPERSTARS 2024

I was invited back to the Superstars Writing Seminar in Colorado Springs, Colorado. The event takes place every February, and it gathers career-focused, professional writers.

I wrote last year that it was the best writing conference I have ever been to. It had the right balance of a great community, helpful information, and useful networking. Usually, a conference only offers one of those three.

Superstars is a jam-packed symphony of a conference, one that I was proud to be invited back to.

In 2024, I will be doing a lot more at the conference. They definitely work their speakers harder than at any conference I've ever been to. Here is what is on my plate:

- a three-hour workshop on writing craft
- a 45-minute presentation on mental models for writers
- an hour-long presentation on elevating your writer's mindset
- eight (8) 15-minute career counseling sessions with aspiring writers

- a VIP dinner in which I host a table of six to seven writers, entertain them, and give writing advice
- possibly a panel or two

Wow, that's one busy conference.

As soon as I knew what was expected of me for 2024, I began planning. If I wasn't careful, the conference would sneak up on me. This wasn't the usual conference where I show up for a two- to three-day conference, give two presentations, and go home. From the moment I step off the plane, I have to go to work. Therefore, this conference, more than any other conference I have spoken at, requires me to be at the top of my game in organization, planning, and execution.

I began preparing for this conference in October 2023. I didn't create any content; rather, I sketched out everything I needed to do, and I used the month to think about and refine my topics.

In November, I began creating content. I started with the three-hour presentation. Three hours is a long time. I've done eight-hour presentations, but somehow, a three-hour presentation seems harder. With eight hours, you have the entire day, which, honestly, is too much time. You have to fill it with breaks and you have to be really intentional about your pacing and the amount of content that you facilitate. But even if you make a mistake, eight hours is a long time; by the end of the day, even if you run out of content and finish early, participants won't be too upset.

Sure, it takes way more time to prepare an eight-hour presentation, and sure, it might seem more intimidating, but I can assure you that three hours is way worse. With three hours, you have to time and pace your content perfectly. My session was in the morning, and there were other sessions planned after mine, so participants were likely to still be fresh-minded when they finished my workshop.

To make the content preparation process easier, I had to break this talk into four 40-minute parts. I'm a big fan of taking a break at regular intervals, so I planned for five-minute breaks for people to use the restroom, check text messages, and stretch.

Then, I began the process of creating the PowerPoint slide deck. The process wasn't too bad. When I am creating slides, I budget for three hours for every finished hour I have to present. Therefore, the three-hour workshop should take me approximately 12 hours to prepare for, though realistically, the number is likely to be closer to 16 to account for rework and last-minute changes.

The topic of the workshop was called "Sharpening Your Writer's Third Eye." It focused on helping participants see the techniques that mega best-selling authors use to keep their readers engaged. The workshop built on many observations I've made while reading the works of mega bestsellers.

The PowerPoint presentation was approximately 60 slides, and there were also exercises. I pulled off some unusual Power-Point techniques. First, I found a way to put timers in slides. When it was time to take a break, I could just click on the timer, and it would begin counting down. That way, participants always knew how much time was left on the clock. That worked beautifully.

Next, I used countdown timers for various exercises I had participants do. I put instructions on the screen in the timer next to the instructions. That worked well too.

The final, coolest thing I did with the PowerPoint were unique images. Since the works of mega bestsellers are copyrighted, I can't share them. However, I can share a summary. But a written summary would be boring. That's what most people would do. Instead, I created a color coding system that expresses a great deal of information instead of a summary. I called it an "x-ray." An x-ray is an analysis of the page that shows dialogue, narrative, and character voice. By looking at an x-ray, you can instantly tell what the mega bestseller is doing on the page. I prepared around 20 x-rays for the workshop, and I happen to think they're pretty cool. We'll see if the participants find them helpful.

Anyway, it took me a week to prepare the workshop, exercises, and visuals. Once I finished that, I breathed a sigh of relief. I did *not* want to be the guy who waited a week before the conference to do his slides. Now I won't be! (And for good measure, I backed up my slides to Backblaze and an external hard drive just to make sure no unfortunate circumstances would befall my slides.)

Preparing the solo presentations on mental models for writers and elevating your writers mindset were a lot easier by comparison. The development process for these talks was unremarkable.

After that, I was finally done, and it was only November 15! I still had around three months left to refine my slides as needed. And refine I did, because I revisited my workshop slides at least three or four times before the end of the year.

In any case, I am ready for the conference and looking forward to connecting with old and new friends again.

BECOME A TECHNOLOGY
AND DATA-DRIVEN WRITER

WALKING THE STREETS OF TOKYO

I'll discuss my adventures in fitness later in this volume, but I did an interesting experiment for a week.

I want to lose weight. I have all the tools I need to be successful; I just need to implement them. One of these tools is a treadmill that I can wheel under my desk to walk while I work. My wife bought it for me as a gift two years ago, but it has been gathering dust. I was currently between books and didn't have anything I was passionate about writing. I didn't have any audiobooks I was actively listening to at the time either.

I decided to challenge my creativity. On a recent trip to Chicago, I went to a gym at my hotel. This gym had Life Fitness treadmills, the kind with screens. The screens display a scenic location in the first-person point of view so that you feel as if you are walking through the place as you work out. As you increase your speed on the treadmill, the pacing of the video increases too. It's pretty cool technology. Every day for a few days, I hiked the trail somewhere in Utah. Pretty cool!

I thought: why not try that at home? I've seen YouTube videos where people do nothing but strap a GoPro to their head and walk. I figured I could create an air sats Life Fitness experience in the comfort of my own home!

Here's how I did it. I wheeled the treadmill under my desk and raised my desk to standing height so that my monitor was placed at eye level. I found a YouTube video of someone walking the streets of Tokyo. I put the video in full screen and put on my AirPods. I synchronized the treadmill with the pace of the person walking in the video so that it felt like I was walking the streets of Shibuya!

It worked beautifully. For an entire week, I got to know the streets of one of the largest and most eccentric cities in the world, one that I've always wanted to visit. I pretended as if I was there. I also did my usual experiment of capturing the place and the five senses. Well, I couldn't exactly capture it in the five senses—I took some creative liberties with smell and taste. But touch, sight, and sound? I gathered a ton of details.

Because I like to complicate things even further, I strapped on my voice recorder and lapel mic and spoke the sensory details I noticed as I walked. This helped me capture them in the moment, though I captured them somewhat inelegantly because my imagery could have been stronger.

Overall, this was a fruitful exercise and I will try it again. It's a great way to defeat the monotony of walking on a treadmill and feeling like a hamster.

REVIEWING A (FAILED) AI GRAMMAR CHECKER

I discovered a new AI grammar checker that uses OpenAI's large language models to edit text. The selling point of the software is that it takes care of the technical, programmatic issues for you like chunking your text and fixing unusual errors with the API.

I was intrigued because this app set out to solve the exact problem that I discussed in previous volumes of this series. The cold truth is that AI grammar checking is available to any author who wants to experiment with it. The catch is that you are at the whims of the OpenAI API. OpenAI is constantly changing its APIs. They retire models, revise existing models, and introduce new models all the time. I've heard many developers complain about the inconsistency of their models. I have seen this inconsistency for myself, and it is problematic. If you're a developer, you want to build a program on a solid foundation. In other words, you need an API that will give you a consistent range of answers.

It's like when you buy gravel at a landscaping store. You don't want a bag of gravel that has different sizes. You want the gravel to be about the same size. The same goes with land-scaping rocks, dirt, and anything that you buy in bulk.

Fast food restaurants wouldn't be where they are if every time you purchased an order of fries, it looked and/or tasted different. Therefore, consistency is important. I don't think OpenAI has figured this out yet, but they will.

Anyway, I wanted to test this new app to see if this developer had figured out something that my developer and I couldn't. It had also been a few months since I had surveyed the current landscape of AI grammar checkers, so I wanted to know if there have been improvements.

(Before we continue, I am not going to name the app I tested. Spoiler alert that it wasn't bad—but these apps come and go very rapidly.)

First, the developer did a good job with this app. Though it was web-based, it functioned very well and did a good job of helping the user create a secret API key with OpenAI. The entire setup process took approximately two minutes. My hat goes off to the developer for this because it is not exactly easy to explain API keys to the average person.

Once the API key is set up, the user enters a string of text, hits enter, and waits as the application runs the text through the OpenAI API and returns results. The shorter the text, the faster the results take and the more accurate they are. The longer the text is, the more opportunities the API has to screw up.

To test the app, I started with a paragraph from my work in progress. I bastardized it with several errors that I know GPT for sure could catch. It caught them all. That made me smile. But the skeptic in me knew that not all was right with the world.

I then took my entire current chapter from my work in progress and pasted it into the program. The editing process took approximately two minutes, and it caught almost none of the errors that were present in the text. In fact, GPT-4 thought that the entire second half of the chapter should have been deleted. Serious fail.

I performed various tests on the program and found that, unfortunately, it suffered from the same problems that my own homebrew application suffered from. These problems are not the fault of the developer. They are the fault of OpenAI. Until they come to their senses, developers everywhere across all spectrums of applications are at the mercy of a company that may or may not have their best interests at heart. This is why I did not proceed with full-scale development of my AI grammar checker. It's helpful for me personally, but the results are too varied.

I like that this developer offered the application to the public, though. I'm a fan of authors seeing what is possible with this new technology. I don't think that this app will be around for more than a year, though. I suspect the developer will learn his lesson, carry the knowledge over to a new AI project, and move on.

The pricing of this application is quite attractive. It's $29 for lifetime access, plus whatever fees you have to pay to OpenAI for the use of the API. Not bad, and in line with what I was thinking of charging for my application.

OpenAI problems aside, the only real downside of this application is that it does not export your text as a Microsoft Word document. It eliminates all paragraphing, and it's up to you to identify where the errors are. The app highlights them in red, but it's not always easy to see.

If an app like this is to be successful, it must have the capability to accept a text file as an input and output a similar text file with all the formatting preserved. Otherwise, it becomes yet another step in the writing process. Writers already have enough steps in the writing process.

Ultimately, this needs to be an add-on feature in the writing apps that writers already use if this technology is to take off.

Still, I always love testing AI grammar checkers. They're a glimpse into the future.

AI EDITING WITH DRAFTSMITH

Earlier this year, I was contacted by Intelligent Editing, the makers of PerfectIt. They were working on a new product that they wanted advice on—a product that used AI to help authors edit their manuscripts. They contacted me because they had worked with me before and saw a video on my channel where I suggested that AI editing was the future and that this future was already here for developers brave enough to create an application based on this technology. I had discovered that one could use the OpenAI API and, with very little prompting, could get it to edit text for typos. The results were better than the current spelling and grammar checkers on the market. I put the idea out there, and it connected.

The Intelligent Editing team showed me a beta version of a program they were working on called Draftsmith. Draftsmith allows users to perform the following edits on their text:

- editing for typos
- editing for polish (a la Grammarly)
- editing for sentence structure

I provided feedback to the team, wished them luck, and didn't think anything else of it.

Six months later, the team reached out and told me they were ready to launch the app. They granted me early access and an extended license in exchange for an honest review.

I am a fan of the Intelligent Editing team. I've been trying to get more authors to use PerfectIt for the last few years because it truly can help authors create more polished manuscripts. It is an essential part of my editing workflow. So, I knew that Draftsmith would be good. However, I was blown away!

Draftsmith is *everything* I wanted in an AI editing app. It uses the power of the OpenAI API, produces consistent results, and integrates directly into Microsoft Word, where I do all of my writing and editing. In other words, I felt like they designed the app for me! Technically, they did because I provided a lot of feedback, but that's beside the point.

I grinned from ear to ear as I tested the app for the first time. It helped me catch typos that I missed during my self-editing sessions. It also caught many errors that Grammarly did not. When combined with Grammarly, Draftsmith helped me create a cleaner manuscript than I could have done on my own. Most importantly, it allows me to retire my AI editing app in favor of a more convenient solution. Now, I can do all of my writing and editing directly inside Microsoft Word.

Other writers are using Microsoft Word to draft and self-edit their manuscripts. They may be using Grammarly or ProWritingAid as well, but they are getting the advanced and more accurate results that the OpenAI API provides. Therefore, my manuscripts will always be cleaner, and it will take me less time to get to that point. I've achieved the ultimate efficiency as a writer. It's an amazing feeling!

Anyway, Draftsmith is an incredible innovation that I hope

people will use. I will be promoting it on my YouTube channel and leveraging my network of contacts to spread the word.

Did I mention that Draftsmith does not retain your text, and it does not use user data to train any AI models? Did I also mention that AI editing does not infringe on anyone's copyright, so therefore, there is no risk of committing copyright infringement like there is with AI art and AI writing software? I told you, this is a slam dunk. I'm glad I'm not the only person who recognized this opportunity.

In any case, I'm thrilled to have achieved peak efficiency in my editing process. My hope is that I've played a small part in helping other authors do the same.

RETURNING TO FICTION
AUDIOBOOK NARRATION

This quarter, I decided to return to making audiobooks. I described in a previous chapter my endeavors and self-narrating the audiobook for my book *The Pocket Guide to Pantsing*, but I also returned to hiring a narrator.

The last audiobook I produced was *The Author Heir Handbook*, narrated by Craig Van Ness. Craig was an absolute professional, and working with him was a pleasure. However, *The Author Heir Handbook* was a nonfiction book, and nonfiction is another animal entirely when it comes to audiobook narration. Fiction is far more challenging, complicated, and expensive. It also follows a different process.

The exorbitant cost of audiobooks is one reason why I have been reluctant to produce audiobooks at scale. *One book* can cost thousands of dollars. Narrating a series could damn well launch you into five figures.

But when it's time, it's time. I settled on producing audiobooks for my *Chicago Rat Shifter* series, a trilogy that I completed in 2022. The series is complete and I have no plans to revisit the world. That made it a perfect candidate for audiobook narration. Also, as my most recent fiction series, the trilogy encapsulates my current ability as a writer. (I've written in previous volumes of the series how audiobooks perform the delightful trick of making *any* author sound like a far better writer than they are because a skilled narrator will intrinsically make up for any deficiencies in the text through excellent narration. But I digress.)

First, I set a budget and determined how much I was willing to spend. I then searched for narrators that met those criteria. Unfortunately, none of my previous narrators had the voice I was looking for, so I had to start from scratch.

I posted the book on the Audible Creation Exchange (ACX) and described what I was looking for. I had to be very careful with the chapter I selected because it needed to encompass the spirit of the series while also giving me a good opportunity to hear what the narrator could do. I selected an early chapter in the book that contained witty banter between the main character Cyrus and his sister, Becca. Cyrus is the protagonist, but Becca is also crucial to the series. In fact, I knew that if the narrator couldn't get Becca right, then the audiobook series wouldn't work. Becca was that important. Therefore, I needed a narrator who was equally adept at male *and* female voices.

The downside to audiobook narration is that many narrators don't always do a good job of representing male and female voices. It's quite rare to find a narrator who can do both convincingly and equally well so that readers don't cringe every time a male voices a female and vice versa. Even professional audiobook narrators don't always get this right. I find that some male narrators inflect their voices upward too much when voicing women; this has the effect of making female characters sound too weak and feeble, which often does not match the author's intent. With female narrators voicing males, the opposite is true. They sometimes deepen their voices so much that it makes me want to laugh because no man I've ever met sounds like that.

This causes the reader to not take the male characters seriously, which also does not reflect the author's intent most of the time. Therefore, it's a delicate, delicate balance, and as an author, you have to develop an ear for the right voice. This is one of the major reasons why narrating fiction audiobooks is drastically different from nonfiction. With nonfiction, the narrator simply reads the text and shares the information within; with fiction, the narrator must perform the text, but they can't perform the text so much that it is like a theater production. On a scale, the performance level should be around a six or seven—enough to make the words form pictures in the reader's head but not enough to dramatize the events. This is difficult to describe in text, but when you produce enough audiobooks, you develop an intrinsic understanding of this paradox.

Within hours of posting *Dead Rat Walking*, I received dozens of auditions. I'm still blown away by the audiobook production process. It never gets old hearing complete strangers read something that you've written. I was humbled that so many people took the time to read the three-page sample and provide their best reading of it.

There is definitely a bell curve distribution with audiobook narration auditions. This is not scientific, but 60 percent of the narrators who auditioned were just fine. They weren't outstanding; they weren't awful. They were just fine. In other words, I could have settled for any of them and they would have produced a serviceable audiobook. However, settling is never good when it comes to audiobook narration.

Twenty percent of these narrators were not good. I wouldn't wish their narration upon my enemies. I say that with much love and respect.

The remaining 20 percent, however, warrant special attention. There were three narrators who stood above and beyond the others. I knew it within ten seconds of listening to the narration. These narrators took the time to truly understand the characters and the text. These were exactly the narrators I was looking for. It devastated me not to be able to pick all three of them.

Runner-up number two did a great job with the sibling banter. His only shortcomings were that he had a slight regional accent that didn't quite jibe with my vision of the characters, and his audio quality was slightly worse than the other two. However, his audio quality was still excellent.

Runner-up number one delivered a flawless performance and I had no criticisms for him other than that the timbre of his voice wasn't as good as the narrator I selected. I liked runner-up number one so much that I asked for his contact information to potentially voice another series in my portfolio in the future. In other words, he was so good that I didn't simply want to cut him loose. I wanted to keep in touch and also be a fan and listen to future audiobooks he produced. He was that good.

And that brings us to the narrator I selected. I knew he was the right guy within ten seconds. I can't explain it; I just knew. He interpreted the characters exactly as I heard them in my head. His interpretation of Cyrus captured my hero completely. He also voiced Becca perfectly in that I didn't question how his tone shifted when he went into female mode. His was the most convincing Becca voice audition. In his voice, I also heard the potential to voice the other characters in the series. This was incredibly important because I have to choose someone who can do *the entire series* based on a five-minute sample. This is why you don't want to get this type of decision wrong, if you can help it.

Once I knew the narrator was the one, I made him an offer. We hopped on a quick phone call and discussed payment terms, timeline, and other logistic items such as the contract. Then, I sent him the contract I had developed for my estate planning series with some modifications. Producing *The Author Estate Handbook* and *The Author Heir Handbook* paid off dividends here because I applied the knowledge from those books to this one.

The contract covered important items such as payment, how to handle overage and underage in the final narration, and several tables that laid out all the terms we discussed by phone. I went through it painstakingly and made sure every term was exactly as we discussed. Once the narrator signed the contract digitally, it was time to begin the great audiobook paper chase.

More so than any other task in the writing world, audiobook narration is an exercise in paperwork and due diligence. Here were the items that I needed to settle before the work could begin:

- A written contract between me and the narrator outlining the terms of the production.
- The ACX contract so that the book could be distributed on Audible and Amazon.
- SAG-AFTRA union paperwork, since the narrator belonged to the union. I had to fill out a series of forms, sign up for an account on the union's payment website, and file all payment arrangements with the union.
- W-9 paperwork for tax purposes, since the narrator is an independent contractor and I would be paying him far more than the $600 threshold required for taxes. Because I would be paying him in 2023 and 2024, I would have to issue 1099 forms in 2024 and 2025 tax years. I had to start planning for that now.
- ISBNs. I had to register ISBNs for each book in the series; one for normal audiobook distribution

channels and another for the library audiobook distribution channel.

- I had to commission audiobook covers from my cover designer because I did not order them upfront when I ordered the e-book and paperback covers.
- I had to prepare the manuscript for the narrator and create a character and pronunciation guide. The character guide gave the narrator a sense of who the characters were and my vision for them. The pronunciation guide covered some non-obvious words with unique pronunciations. Fortunately, this story didn't have many character names or pronunciations that needed special attention.
- Rejections to narrators I didn't select.

I delivered a quick and detailed rejection to the narrators I did not select for the project. I'm a big believer in doing this. As an author, I often send my work out into the world and receive no explanation as to why it isn't selected for one thing or another. Magazine editors almost never reply about a short story submission; readers never tell you why they don't like one of your books. Marketing and promotion sites never tell you why they turned down one of your books for promotion. And so on. I believe it is good karma and common decency to reply to audiobook narration auditions. It's just the right thing to do. Anyway, I listened to every audition, good or bad, and I replied with a hearty thank you and the reason the audiobook narrator did not get the job. For some, they just weren't the right fit. Their voice didn't match my vision and it was as easy as that. For others, their audio quality was terrible and I told them that in no uncertain terms. One narrator sounded so quiet, I could barely hear him. I told him he might want to look into that. Another narrator sent me raw and unfinished audio, which is customary for auditions because it doesn't make sense to master audition audio, but his raw audio was extremely bad. When I told him this, he replied and said that every narrator sends raw audio. I replied again and told him that while this was true, his raw audio was worse than everybody else's and that he may want to double-check the assumptions about his audio settings.

In all cases, all of the narrators were pleasant, cordial, and they thanked me for replying. They told me that almost no one does this, and while they didn't get the job, they sincerely appreciated hearing feedback. Though I had to deliver some tough news, that made me feel good about my decision to provide a personal reply.

However, the hardest replies of all were to the runners-up. I could have easily selected either of them to narrate the book, but I had to give them a solid reason why they were not selected. That was a lot harder.

Anyway, once the rejection and paperwork were done, it was time to wait.

The narrator provided the first 15 minutes of the audiobook for my review, and I provided feedback. He did an excellent job. Hearing the first 15 minutes confirmed that I had picked the right guy. Several weeks later, the narrator sent me the finished and mastered audiobook, and I forwarded that to a freelancer I work with who does audiobook proofing (also something I perfected in producing my last round of audiobooks). She provided a list of timestamps for any part that didn't match the text exactly or where there were vocal artifacts. This narrator made almost no mistakes. That's what it's like to work with a pro.

We then promptly moved on to the next book, which was a lot faster and easier to produce because all the paperwork was already in place. The contract addressed the entire series so we didn't have to execute another one; all of the union paperwork was also settled.

Overall, the narrator did an outstanding job. When it was time to publish the audiobooks, I published them on ACX, Findaway Voices, Authors Republic, and on my website. I also released *Dead Rat Walking* on my YouTube channel for my 46,000 subscribers. My hope was that they would listen and buy the other books in the series. Audiobooks are difficult to market, so you have to use every tool at your disposal!

Honestly, I wish I was at a point in my career where making an audiobook edition for each book I published was a foregone conclusion. I love this process so much and would love nothing more than to do it for all of my books. One day, I'll get there.

LOOKING FORWARD

FOCUSING ON FITNESS

This isn't a chapter on writing per se, but it does impact my writing.

I mentioned in the previous volume of this series that I am focusing on my health. I made a commitment to losing weight, eating better, and living a more active lifestyle. This chapter will focus on actions I've taken to improve my fitness because they have improved almost every area of my life.

I was never someone who went to the gym often. I had a streak in 2012 and 2013 when I went to the gym religiously, but for various reasons, I stopped. This was unfortunate, because I gained a lot of weight.

Up until college, I was relatively fit. I never had many muscles, but I participated in marching band all four years of high school, a sport that requires a lot of movement. I never wore a pedometer during my marching band practices, but if I did, I wouldn't have been surprised if I logged more than 10,000 steps *per practice session*. People in marching bands move. A lot. Anyway, when you're lugging heavy saxophones and sousaphones around for four hours a day, it makes a big difference in your level of fitness.

I miss those marching band days. I took for granted at the time what a tremendous favor band was doing for my health. It is only now, 20 years later, that I truly understand that value. If I ever have the time to go back into a marching band, I would seriously consider it for this reason alone.

Anyway, when I went to college, I walked everywhere, which was great for my fitness, but it wasn't the same. Slowly, my life became more sedentary, and slowly, I picked up the pounds. I also picked up high cholesterol and blood pressure, and I realized that I had to make some changes.

I decided that from now on, I will integrate writing with movement. In a previous volume in the series, I talked about how I wrote my *Chicago Rat Shifter* series while on an exercise bike. I lost ten pounds while writing *Dead Rat Walking*. There was something about being in a state of movement while writing that energized me. If it were true that I could lose ten pounds while writing a novel, what if I wrote *all* of my novels in some state of movement? Whether it's walking my dog, walking on a treadmill, sitting on an exercise bike, or something else— wouldn't those benefits reverberate into other areas of my life and health?

I don't know for sure, but I have a hard time imagining that doing this *wouldn't* be beneficial to me.

Thus, I began the long process of making writing and moving simultaneously a habit. I already dictate my novels when I walk my dog; the real challenge would be to move while I am at my desk. When I am at my desk, my brain associates writing with sitting or standing. I suspected that this would take a long time to make second nature, and it did. It took me approximately two months of writing while moving every day to make it a habit. Now I don't think about it anymore. It's just a part of my lifestyle. It's just a part of who I am. I don't overdo it, and I don't write *every time* I am at my desk. But many times I am at my desk, I am moving. My brain has made the connection, and I hope this will be beneficial for my health.

As I said, I have never been a gym rat. I don't intend to become one. But I did purchase a gym membership to increase my options and add variety, especially in the winter. I started buying every fitness book I could. I read bodybuilding books, nutrition books, conspiracy theory books about different types of foods that some doctors think are evil, and so on. I ventured deep into the fitness and nutrition worlds, just like I did when I delved into the world of self-publishing in 2012. There is so much to learn, and I haven't even scratched the surface yet.

There are so many workout videos on YouTube for free. Seriously, it's astonishing. At first, I thought I would have to purchase a subscription to various workout routines, but that was silly. There were thousands of workout videos in my pocket all along! Once I discovered that, I learned more about workout routines. You see, the only workout routines I had watched in my life up until that point were from Richard Simmons when I was in elementary school. Those PE classes where we had to dance to Richard Simmons were torturous and I bitched and moaned every minute of them, but honestly, if I could go back in time, I probably would've taken them more seriously. You can bet that I was watching Richard Simmons workouts on YouTube to make up for it!

I found lots of different trainers and lots of different workout and calisthenics routines. I went in with no preconceived notions and I tried every single one. I gave every single trainer a chance. Granted, I couldn't do all of the workouts because I'm not yet in shape, but every trainer had something to teach me. Men, women, yoga instructors, bodybuilders, calisthenics instructors, Pilates teachers, and more. I found this journey fascinating.

I learned many different types of stretches, warm-up

routines, cooldown routines, and so on. I watched endless muscled YouTube macho men giving their advice on the best workout strategies. They often contradicted each other.

I watched endless fit women in sports bras and yoga pants giving *their* best advice, which also often was contradictory too. In short, I entered the land of fitness with the eyes (and naiveté) of a child. That's what you have to do when you're committed to truly making a change in your life. You can't have any judgment. You can't have any preconceived notions. You can't claim to know anything other than your own personal limits, which, depending on the circumstances, may also be malleable. You just have to be a sponge and be willing to soak up everything. You can decide what to keep or throw out later. But for me, I just needed to move. It didn't matter how I moved. I just needed to go for it.

I still haven't found a solid workout routine just yet. I'm still working on my goals. I've hired a personal trainer to help me at the gym. I don't have anything to conclude this chapter with other than that I am doing it, and that matters. And it feels great.

It took only a week to reap the benefits of daily workouts. I noticed that if I worked out first thing in the morning, I felt great for the rest of the day. In fact, I noticed such a difference that I didn't *not* want to work out in the mornings. That in and of itself is a victory.

So begins my commitment to fitness. It has helped me have more energy during my writing sessions, get more done in my day, and I feel great doing it.

FOCUSING ON NUTRITION

I have also been focusing on nutrition recently. I am a decent eater. I'm not picky about food. My list of "do not touch" foods is quite brief:

- artichokes
- hearts of palm
- mustard
- extremely hot peppers for very hot hot sauce
- pig's feet

That's it. I will eat just about anything else. Sure, I like some foods more or less than others, but I'm an easy guy when it comes to food. That has been one of my problems in life. I enjoy food; I don't have an unhealthy relationship with it, but I can be better at moderation.

I began working with a nutritionist who is a registered dietitian. Together, we looked at what I was eating and how it was contributing to my weight gain in general unhealthiness. When I ate well, I ate well, but I was never mindful about portion sizes. I also was a serial snacker. I was also guilty of eating maybe a little too much fat due to convenience. After all, I have a busy lifestyle and I don't always have time to cook, especially when traveling. So, I was guilty of all charges there.

My nutritionist and I worked out a plan to slowly introduce new foods into my diet that I can eat without taking away anything. I learned about portion sizes, how to read a food label properly, and how to make simple changes at the grocery store. I know all of this sounds silly and many people would probably shake their heads at such statements, but that's the state of many Americans. Nutrition is just not a focus in this culture. In fact, I would argue that just about everything at the grocery store is trying to kill you.

Case in point about the grocery store trying to kill you: just because something says "heart healthy" or "fat-free," that doesn't mean a damn thing. Companies know that people make emotional reactions when at the grocery store. These companies also know that people very seldom read the food labels. And even when they do, the food labels often don't make any sense. When you read an ingredient list, do you know what the chemicals are? If a label says "canola oil," many people eat canola oil and are fine with it. But if something says "expressed propeller canola oil," most people have no idea what that is and why it is better for you. When people grab a jar of peanut butter, they don't care whether it has hydrogenated oils and it. They are not going to know what those are. For that reason, the cards are stacked against you when you shop at the grocery store unless you do your research. Most people don't have time for that. I myself was in that camp for 35 years. But now that I have gotten some advice and know a thing or two about the various ingredients in food, I have learned what I've been truly putting into my body over the years. My only solace is that I figured all of this out before I had a major health meltdown, and my only hope is that it is not too late. But I digress.

The first two or three weeks of adjusting to my nutritionist's advice was mostly not unceremonious. I ate a few extra things here, reduced a few portions there, and life. I didn't notice any changes.

However, after the third week, I noticed some substantial changes (in addition to the fact that I had been getting more exercise). I noticed that if I worked out in the morning and had a breakfast with at least 30 grams of protein, I felt amazing for the rest of the day. And when I say amazing, I mean I had as much energy as I had when I was 18. I felt like a teenager again. At first, I wasn't sure what to think about this transformation. I chalked it up to great weather outside, non-stressful days at work, and great progress on the book I was working on. However, the weather turned sour, work became a lot more stressful, and I finished that book. The high energy levels remained.

I kept up the routine. My energy levels never flagged. I had so much energy, I didn't know what to do with it. I realized what I had failed to realize for 35 years: food is fuel. Again, I know it sounds silly, but sometimes you have to learn and relearn things throughout your life multiple times before they sink into your thick skull.

I had stopped eating processed foods almost entirely, doubled and tripled my whole food and vegetable intake, and made entirely different choices at the grocery store. I was eating food that I really liked. I was not on a "diet." I was just simply eating nutritious food that was fueling me. It has made such a difference that I don't know how I can ever go back.

I love having such abundant energy. It makes me more creative and productive.

Anyway, that's my focus on nutrition this quarter. It's going to serve me incredibly well in my life.

2023 is now over. Like 2022, it was a good year but not a great year. Honestly, 2023 was worse than 2022, and my results a disappointing upon reflecting on them.

That said, I still made a ton of progress toward my goals and I can celebrate a few wins before 2024 begins.

BECOME A WRITING MASTER

To achieve my goal of becoming a writing master, I will focus on the following tactical priorities:

- Demonstrate a commitment to learning the craft of story-telling and teaching
- Demonstrate a commitment to outstanding quality AND quantity

Examples of day-to-day activities that will help me carry out my tactical priorities include:

- Keep learning through online courses and workshops taught by professional writers who are further down the path I want to walk
- Reading
- Developing mentorships
- Finding new ways to increase my daily word counts
- Mastering different writing methods
- Documenting my process of becoming a successful writer in the *Indie Author Confidential* series
- Cleaning up my platform to ensure a consistent quality reader experience

What did I do to become a writing master during Q4 2023?

1. I changed this strategic priority from "Become a World-Class Content Creator" to "Become a Writing Master," which more accurately reflects my true goals.
2. I continued my relationship with my mentor acquired last year.
3. I bounced back from a bad illness, and that in of itself is an accomplishment.
4. I read (and studied the craft in) over 20 books by mega bestsellers.
5. I failed in my attempt to reach 100 books by 2024, but I'm not that far away.
6. I produced a fiction audiobook series, adding to my audiobook footprint.
7. I landed two short stories in science fiction and fantasy anthologies, increasing my reach.

BECOME A TECHNOLOGY AND DATA-DRIVEN WRITER

To achieve my goal of becoming a technology and data-driven writer, I will focus on the following tactical priorities:

- Use technology to make the business more efficient
- Use data to get insights
- Examples of day-to-day activities that will help me carry out my tactical priorities include:
- Developing a tax plan
- Developing an estate plan assisted with technology
- Learning how to design my own covers
- Hiring a personal assistant for small tasks where it makes sense
- Developing a metadata database for my work
- Improving my readers' experience on my website
- Implementing direct sales for my fiction

What did I do to become a more technology and data-driven writer during Q4 2023?

1. I developed an AI editing app that helped me decrease the amount of errors in my work.
2. My videos where I shared my thoughts on AI editing resonated with a developer who created the ultimate AI editing tool...which I am now using.
3. I developed a working (and long-lasting) system to keep my email inbox and to-do list under control.
4. I built an ONIX data feed (which is a metadata database) and added a distribution channel where I can reach readers with visual impairments. The

data feed can also be used for future retailer distribution if that ever becomes available, therefore streamlining my book distribution.

As I said, this was a challenging year. I'm glad to see it end. I don't know what 2024 holds, but I'm cautiously optimistic. Regardless, I will keep making progress no matter what happens, and as long as I am healthy enough to do so, that's all that matters.

2024 STRATEGIC PRIORITIES

I am not setting crazy goals for 2024. In fact, I am only setting a few. 2022 and 2023 were difficult enough that I want to start small and work my way back up to where I was in 2021. For that reason, this is going to be an unusually short chapter compared to previous years.

First and foremost, I want to reach 100 books published by December 31, 2024. That is my first priority. I also want to write at least one new fiction series to test out many of the lessons I've been learning from mega bestsellers this year.

Next, I want to focus on marketing and profit more next year than I have in the past. I need to find new revenue streams, find new ways to reach readers, do more active marketing, and so on.

That's it.

From a Become a Writing Master perspective, I am doing all the right things in studying the mega bestsellers and practicing their techniques. I'm exploring a premium writing course that I would like to put together based on my 2024 Superstars presentation "Sharpening Your Writer's Third Eye." I think I can make it very valuable and helpful for authors. Depending on how the presentation is received, I may run with this idea in Q1 2024 while the idea is still hot.

Also, I need to fill my short story well. While I won't be doing the Ray Bradbury challenge, I'll need to write at least 6 stories in 2024 to keep my work in front of all the major magazines and contests.

From a Technology and Data-Driven Writer perspective, I am in an amazing spot. All the work I've done over the past five years has paid off big time. I've achieved efficiency and effectiveness that I only dreamed of. From dictation to AI editing to ChatGPT for sales copy to AI art, I've got the tech and data pieces down cold. As a result, unless something really cool pops up, I will be focusing less on this strategic priority next year. Honestly, I'm having a hard time seeing how I can make more gains in this strategic priority area in 2024. That's good because I can focus more on production and marketing, which will generate more revenue to innovate on levels I wasn't able to previously. For example, I need a new website, but that's not an option until I grow my sales. It's going to be very, very expensive to create the website I need to create to get to the next level of my business.

Even though tech and data are my specialties, it's time to back off of them for a little while. I'll surely dabble in a few things, but production will be my key focus. If I do write tech and data chapters, they are likely to be from a marketing perspective.

For this reason, at least in 2024, most of my chapters in *Indie Author Confidential* will be focused on Become a Writing Master.

So, to summarize, my goals are:

- Achieve milestone of 100 books published by December 31, 2024
- Write 6 short stories for magazines
- Produce a premium writing course (maybe)
- Focus less on tech and data and more on marketing

Let's see how 2024 goes.

READ THE NEXT VOLUME

Michael's writer journey continues in the next volume of this series!

Grab your copy at www.authorlevelup.com/confidential.

MEET M.L. RONN

Science fiction and fantasy on the wild side!

M.L. Ronn (Michael La Ronn) is the author of many science fiction and fantasy novels including *The Good Necromancer*, *Android X,* and *The Last Dragon Lord* series.

In 2012, a life-threatening illness made him realize that storytelling was his #1 passion. He's devoted his life to writing ever since, making up whatever story makes him fall out of his chair laughing the hardest. Every day.

Learn more about Michael
www.authorlevelup.com (for writers)
www.michaellaronn.com (fiction)

MORE BOOKS BY M.L. RONN

Books for Writers:

www.authorlevelup.com/books

Fiction:
www.michaellaronn.com/books